BUILDING BLOCKS OF COMPUTER SCIENCE

ORDER in CODING

Written by Echo Elise González

Illustrated by Graham Ross

a Scott Fetzer company
Chicago

World Book, Inc.
180 North LaSalle Street
Suite 900
Chicago, Illinois 60601
USA

For information about other World Book publications, visit our website at **www.worldbook.com** or call **1-800-WORLDBK (967-5325).**
For information about sales to schools and libraries, call 1-800-975-3250 (United States), or 1-800-837-5365 (Canada).

Library of Congress Cataloging-in-Publication Data for this volume has been applied for.

Building Blocks of Computer Science
ISBN: 978-0-7166-2883-5 (set, hc.)

Order in Coding
ISBN: 978-0-7166-2888-0 (hc.)

Also available as:
ISBN: 978-0-7166-2896-5 (e-book)

1st printing August 2020

STAFF

Executive Committee

President: Geoff Broderick
Vice President, Finance: Donald D. Keller
Vice President, Marketing: Jean Lin
Vice President, International Sales: Maksim Rutenberg
Vice President, Technology: Jason Dole
Director, Editorial: Tom Evans
Director, Human Resources: Bev Ecker

Editorial

Manager, New Content: Jeff De La Rosa
Writer: Echo Elise González
Proofreader: Nathalie Strassheim

Digital

Director, Digital Product Development: Erika Meller
Digital Product Manager: Jon Wills

Graphics and Design

Sr. Visual Communications Designer: Melanie Bender
Coordinator, Design Development and Production: Brenda B. Tropinski
Sr. Web Designer/Digital Media Developer: Matt Carrington

Acknowledgments:
Art by Graham Ross/The Bright Agency
Series reviewed by Peter Jang/Actualize Coding Bootcamp

TABLE OF CONTENTS

There is a glossary on page 30. Terms defined in the glossary are in type **that looks like this** on their first appearance.

ORDER!
Hi! I'm **Control Flow.** You can call me Flow!
I'm the order in which a computer follows the steps of a computer program.
Order is important in a program!
There's no use in writing good lines of code if the order is out of whack.

To get the result that we want...
We must make sure things are put together in the correct order.
Programmers have many tools and methods for ensuring proper order.
They use **data-sorting algorithms** to sort information.
Programmers also keep control flow in mind to make sure their program is organized properly.
Let's take a closer look and see how computer programs go with the flow!

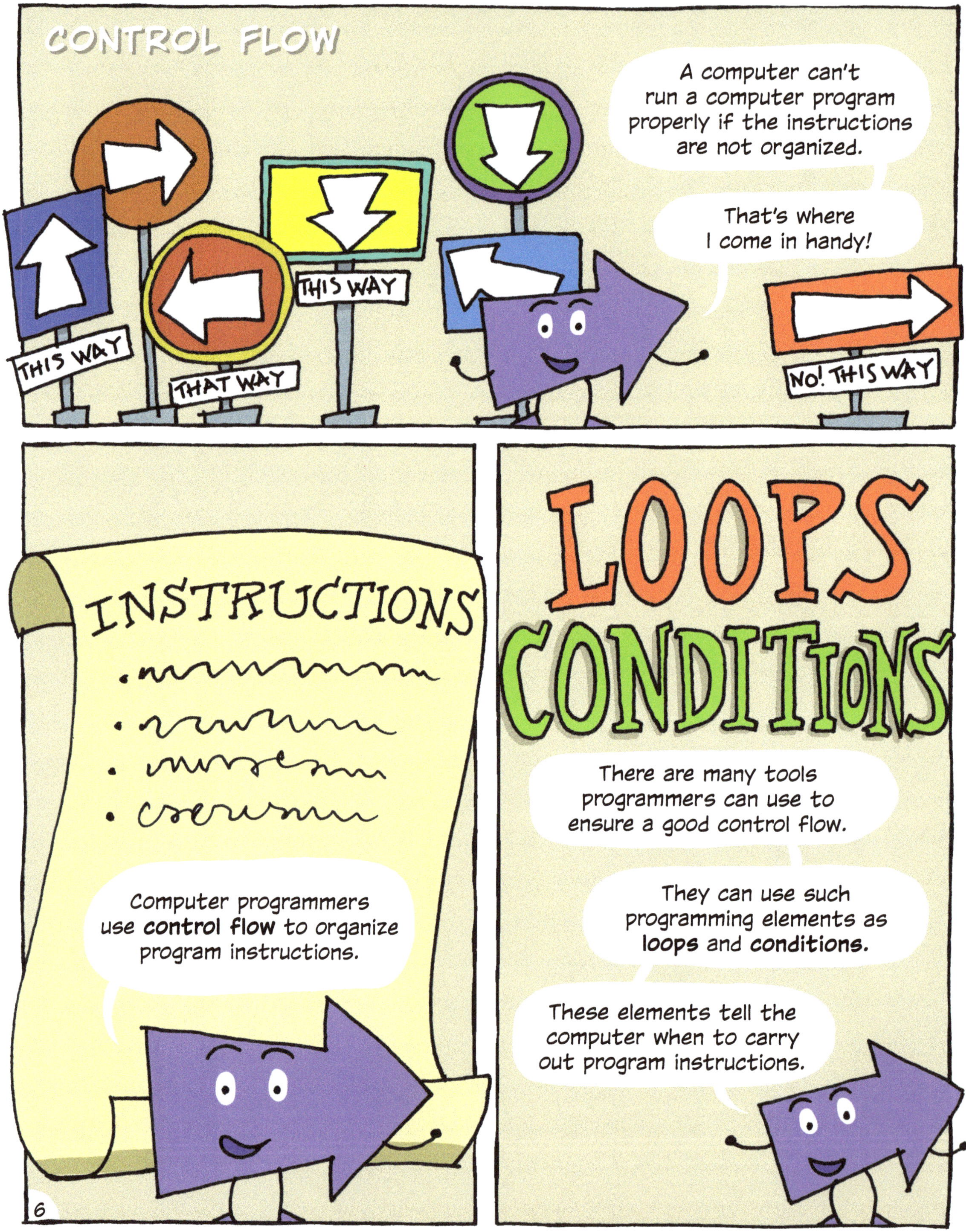

CONTROL FLOW

THIS WAY
THAT WAY
THIS WAY
NO! THIS WAY

A computer can't run a computer program properly if the instructions are not organized.

That's where I come in handy!

LOOPS

CONDITIONS

There are many tools programmers can use to ensure a good control flow.

They can use such programming elements as **loops** and **conditions.**

These elements tell the computer when to carry out program instructions.

Put socks on.

Choose socks.

Tie shoelaces.

Put shoes on.

For example, here are instructions for putting my socks and shoes on.

It looks like they're not in order...

I can't make much sense of them like this!

That's why control flow is important when writing a program.

Using **loops, conditions,** and other coding elements is an important part of **control flow.**

Programmers use these elements to create different kinds of control flow.

The three basic kinds of control flow are called **sequencing, iteration,** and **selection.**
SEQUENCING
ITERATION
SELECTION

Each of these flows enables the computer to run a program in a particular kind of order.

A sequenced control flow simply runs program instructions one step at a time.
An iteration control flow repeats one or more program instructions.
A selection control flow only runs some program instructions when certain conditions are true.
A computer program will usually run in a sequenced order unless the programmer uses program elements to create a different kind of flow.

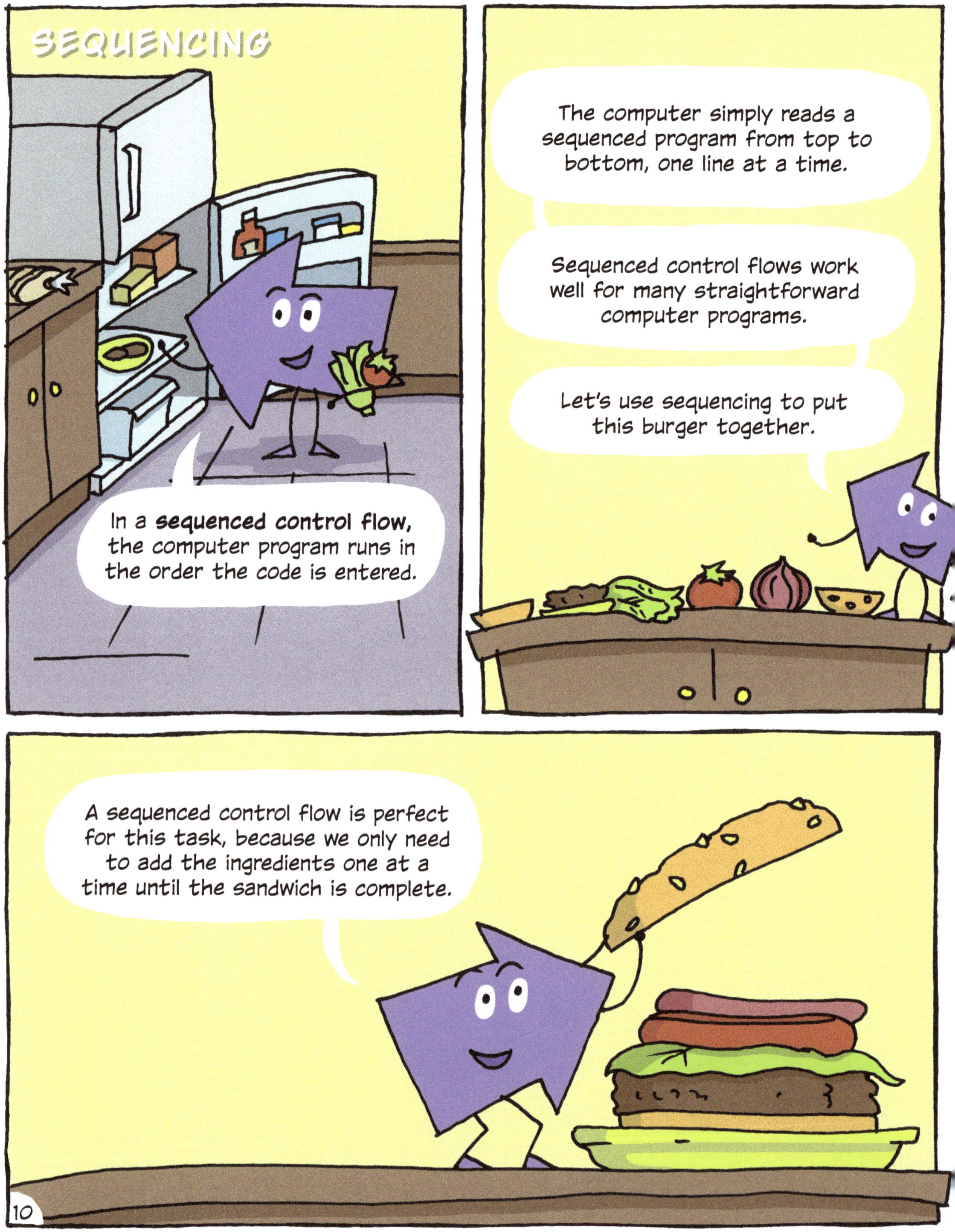

SEQUENCING

The computer simply reads a sequenced program from top to bottom, one line at a time.

Sequenced control flows work well for many straightforward computer programs.

Let's use sequencing to put this burger together.

A sequenced control flow is perfect for this task, because we only need to add the ingredients one at a time until the sandwich is complete.

When hungry
start with bun
add patty
add lettuce
add tomato slice
add onion
finish with bun
If we were writing a burger-making computer program, the computer would simply need to follow the steps one at a time from the beginning to the end...
...until it reached the end of the program.

SELECTION
With **selection,** we can skip over certain lines of code unless a certain **condition** is met.
This will come in handy in controlling the flow of our burger-making program.
Let's say we want to add an option to assemble a vegetarian burger.

We can add a condition that will give us a vegetarian option.
This selection control flow enables us to skip the beef patty and replace it with a veggie patty if we want to.

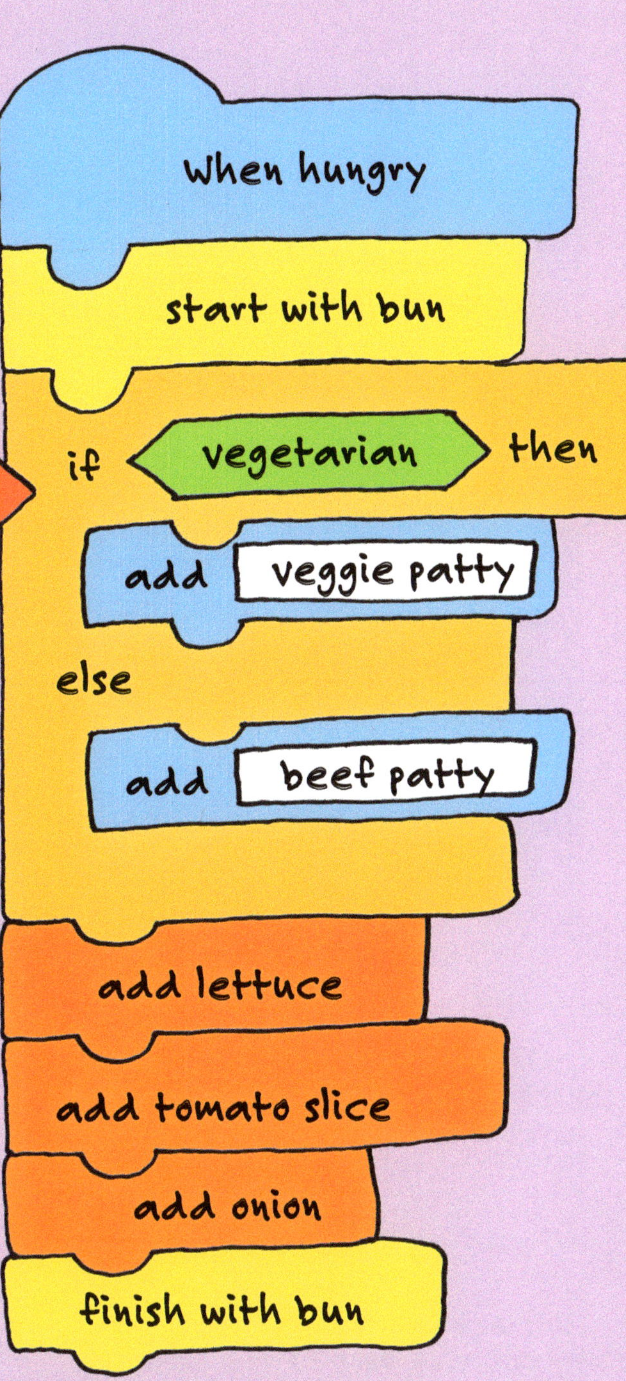
when hungry
start with bun
if vegetarian then
add veggie patty
else
add beef patty
add lettuce
add tomato slice
add onion
finish with bun

I'm hungry.

Let's write a program to eat the hamburger we built!

We can use an **iteration control flow** to make this program.

Here are code blocks for taking a bite, chewing, and swallowing.

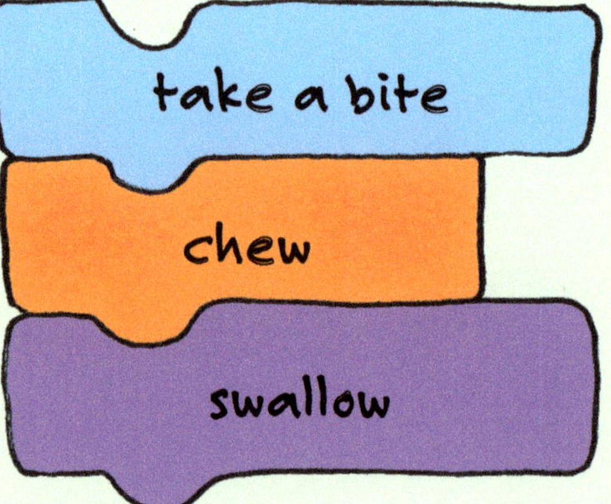

These steps must be done multiple times, over and over again, until the hamburger is finished.

So, let's use iteration to carry out this part of the code as many times as we want.

REPEAT

take a bite

chew

swallow

I'll add a **loop** to repeat this part.

Now, I don't have to add these same blocks over and over again!

Looks like the sandwich-eating program is ready to run!

NOM! NOM! NOM!

DATA SORTING
Order is important not only in how lines of code are organized...
But also in how information is organized within a program.
Let's say we want to give each of these orangutans a balloon.
We want to give them the balloons in order of size, so that the smallest orangutan has the smallest balloon, the biggest orangutan has the biggest balloon, and so on.
It would be easier to do this if we first **sort** the balloons and the orangutans into an order that's useful to us.

So, let's sort both groups in order of size.
Now, we can easily match the balloons to the orangutans by size!

Sorting a list of **data** into a meaningful order is called **data sorting.**
It's my buddy, Al!
Al is an **algorithm.** He helps me keep things nice and orderly.
An algorithm is a step-by-step set of instructions.
Programmers use algorithms to design computer programs.
They write out the algorithms line by line.
Then they can write the steps out in code for a computer to read.
TAP TAP

Algorithms can be used to accomplish just about any kind of task a computer can perform.

Data-sorting algorithms are specifically designed to put lists of information in order.

DICTIONARY

I can find a word in the dictionary because the words are in alphabetical order.

INSERTION SORT
The insertion sort is a common data-sorting algorithm.
In an insertion sort, the elements in a list are sorted one by one.
We take each element out of the list and insert it back in the correct position.
Suppose we have a bunch of baby sea turtles that we want to sort by color.
We want to sort the turtles from greenest to bluest, so that the greenest ones are on the left and the bluest ones are on the right.
We can sort them using an insertion sort.
A
B
C
D
E

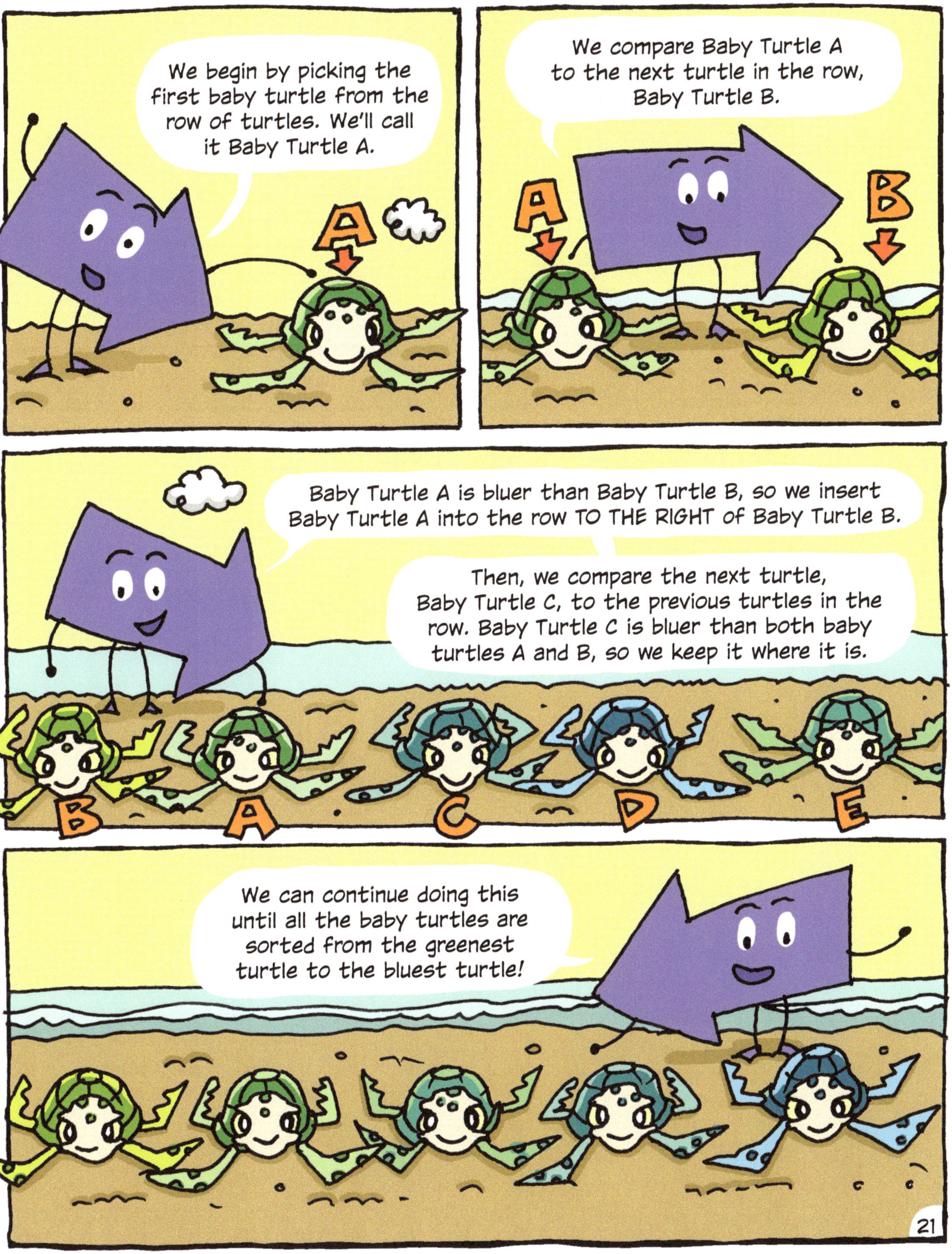

Baby Turtle A is bluer than Baby Turtle B, so we insert Baby Turtle A into the row TO THE RIGHT of Baby Turtle B.

Then, we compare the next turtle, Baby Turtle C, to the previous turtles in the row. Baby Turtle C is bluer than both baby turtles A and B, so we keep it where it is.

B A C D E

We can continue doing this until all the baby turtles are sorted from the greenest turtle to the bluest turtle!

SELECTION SORT
An **algorithm** that is similar to the **insertion sort** is the **selection sort.**
A selection sort also goes through each element in a list one by one.
However, rather than moving each element of the list as it goes, a selection sort always chooses the minimum or maximum element.
Suppose we have a group of giraffes.
Like, a LOT of giraffes...
And we want to put them in order from tallest to shortest.
A selection sort could help us do this.
With a selection sort, we put all of the unsorted giraffes into a big group together.

SORTED AREA
Next, we pick out the tallest giraffe from the group and put it in a new, sorted area.
We then pick the next-tallest giraffe and put it to the right of the tallest giraffe in the new area.
We continue doing this until all of the giraffes have been sorted.

MERGE SORT
Another common type of data-sorting algorithm is the merge sort.
Merge sorting is a bit more complex than selection sorting.
But, it is more useful and efficient in certain situations.
Polly wants a cracker!
Hi.
Let's try using a merge sort to arrange these parrots.
This above all: to thine own self be true. And it must follow, as the night the day, thou canst not then be false to any man...
We want the least talkative parrots to be on the left and the most talkative parrots to be on the right.
Hi.
Polly wants a cracker!
Those friends thou hast, and their adoption tried, Grapple them unto thy soul with hoops of steel,...
With a merge sort, we first divide the group in half.

Hi.
Polly wants a cracker!
But do not dull thy palm with entertainment...
Then, we split each half again and keep repeating until we can't split the groups in half any further.

Hi.
Polly wants a cracker!
Of entrance to a quarrel, but being in,...
So, let's start merging them back together in order from least talkative to most talkative.

Let's compare the first parrots on each branch.
Hi.
Polly wants a cracker!
Give every man thy ear but few thy voice....
The less talkative one will be the first in the ordered row.

Hi.
Polly wants a cracker!
Costly thy habit as thy purse can buy,...
Let's keep comparing the first parrots on each branch...

Polly wants a cracker!
But not expressed in fancy-rich, not gaudy,...
Hi.

Until the birds are arranged from shyest to wordiest!
Polly wants a cracker!
Hi.
For the apparel oft proclaims the man, And they in France of the best rank and station Are of a most select and generous chief in that.

Whether a programmer has to organize a list of items for a video game...
a list of **data** for a **spreadsheet...**
or a list of words for a website...
...a **data-sorting algorithm** can help!
There are many different data-sorting algorithms.

Some use the **divide-and-conquer** method to divide the data and then re-merge it in the correct order.
Others simply compare the data in pairs, over and over, until it's all sorted.
Some involve picking out elements one at a time and re-inserting them in the correct position.
Which sorting method is best depends on the needs of a particular program.

Computer programmers understand the importance of order.
Any good computer program is organized in a way that makes sense both to the programmer writing it and to the computer carrying it out.

Whether we are sorting the **data** that makes up a program...

Or organizing the program itself in a way that produces the result we want...

We always want to go with the flow.

It's all about order!

GLOSSARY

algorithm a set of step-by-step instructions used to write computer programs. Algorithms are also used to solve math problems and other problems.

condition a statement that can be true or false. A program may tell a computer to run a piece of code if a certain condition is true.

control flow the order in which a computer follows the steps of a computer program.

data information that a computer processes or stores.

data sorting sorting a list of data into a particular order.

divide-and-conquer a data-sorting strategy in which data is divided, then recombined in a particular order.

insertion sort a sorting algorithm in which the elements in a list are sorted one by one.

iteration a control flow in which certain lines of code are repeated.

loop a piece of code that causes part of a program to run over and over again.

merge sort a sorting algorithm that splits up the elements in a list into groups and pairs, then recombines them in the correct order.

selection a control flow in which certain lines of code are skipped over unless certain conditions are true.

selection sort a sorting algorithm that goes through the elements in a list one by one, choosing the minimum or maximum element.

sequencing a control flow in which the computer program follows the steps of code in order.

sorting algorithm an algorithm that is used to put a list of data in a particular order.

spreadsheet a document in which data is arranged in rows and columns.

GO ONLINE

Now that you know all about how important order is in coding, you can try sorting some data yourself! Go to this website to find the Sort the Giraffes activity, and many other fun computer science activities!

www.worldbook.com/BuildingBlocks

INDEX

www.ingramcontent.com/pod-product-compliance
Ingram Content Group UK Ltd.
Pitfield, Milton Keynes, MK11 3LW, UK
UKHW061958290726
14090UKWH00021B/1268